The (Really!) Great Barrier Reef

by Tisha Hamilton

Table of Contents

Introduction 2

Chapter 1
The Coral Reef. 5

Chapter 2
Many Habitats 8

Chapter 3
A Valuable Resource 15

Conclusion 18

Glossary and Index 19

Comprehension Check 20

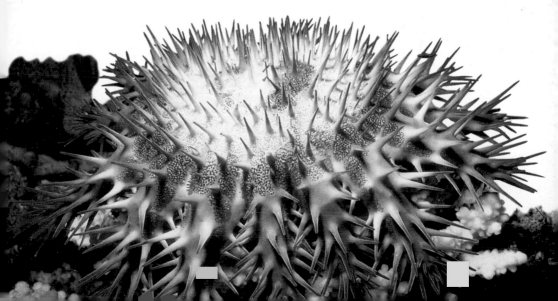

Introduction

A coral reef is a shelf that runs along the coastlines of countries throughout the world. Coral reefs are found in shallow, warm waters all over the world.

Among all these reefs, there is one that stands out. It is the Great Barrier Reef along the coast of Australia. It is remarkable for many reasons. One is its length—over 1,250 miles. It is the largest coral reef **ecosystem** in the world and the largest **organic** structure on the planet. It is also home to numerous kinds of sea life.

☝ The dots on this map indicate where barrier reefs are located.

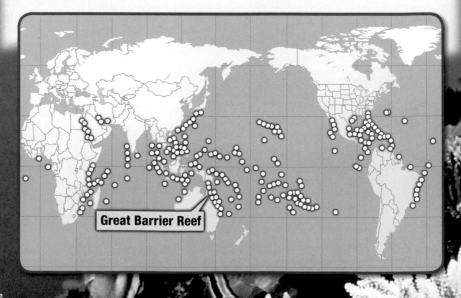

Great Barrier Reef

About 40,000 years ago, the Aboriginal peoples were the only humans living on the Australian continent. They fished and hunted along parts of the Great Barrier Reef. For a long period of time they were the only people who knew the reef existed.

When sailors began to explore the world, their boats sometimes hit the sharp coral that was under the water, sinking their vessels. The reef remained a mystery.

Soft coral polyps ⤴

🎧 This flat-bottomed boat is very similar to the one Captain James Cook used.

That changed in 1769 when the English explorer Captain James Cook sailed to Australia. He knew that a dangerous reef lurked just beneath the water, but he had a plan to get across it.

He sailed over the reef in a special flat-bottomed boat. The bottom of this vessel did not push deep into the water like most boats of the time, so he could safely float over the shallow water. He was the first explorer to see the reef. As he sailed along, he could hardly believe his eyes. What exactly did he see?

CHAPTER 1

The Coral Reef

The words *hard*, *smooth*, *rough*, and *sharp* all describe coral. The words *spiky*, *flat*, *round*, and *bushy* do too. The color of coral ranges from white to deep purple and bright red.

Coral has many shapes and patterns. There are hard, round lumps of brain coral. There are spiky branches of stag horn coral. Other coral is shaped like huge ferns. Some coral grow in wavy rows, in mazes, as tiny stars, or as bumps.

↻ The Great Barrier Reef is as colorful as a rainbow.

So what is true of all coral? Coral is very hard and mostly made up of limestone. Tiny sea animals called polyps make the coral. The polyps convert salt from the ocean waters into **limestone**. The limestone then forms a hard outer shell to protect the polyp's fragile body.

Each polyp grows new polyps. These polyps begin the process again. Picture a shell on top of a shell on top of a shell. That is what coral is like. It is many tiny polyp shells on top of and alongside each other. When polyps die, their limestone shells remain. That is how a coral reef grows.

mouth   tentacle

The Coral Animal

A polyp is a round animal with a mouth in the middle and a ring of tentacles around the mouth.

The Great Barrier Reef Is Ancient

How old is the Great Barrier Reef? Scientists have made estimates ranging from about 20,000 years old to 2 million years old, but most scientists agree that it probably began to form about 500,000 years ago. No matter what the number, the Great Barrier Reef is ancient.

The Great Barrier Reef is not one reef. It is made up of nearly 3,000 smaller reefs with about 400 **species** of coral. Just as the coral forms one on top of the other, so do the many reefs that make up the Great Barrier Reef.

Not all of the Great Barrier Reef is under the water. It is estimated that there are over 900 islands made up of coral. Some of them are **habitable**. Most are not.

◑ Lizard Island is one of the many islands of the Great Barrier Reef.

CHAPTER 2

Many Habitats

The reef has many diverse **habitats**. Birds of all kinds fly above it. They eat its fish, float in its waters, and nest on its islands. Scientists have documented 22 species and have estimated the total bird **population** to be about two million.

Sea turtles, crabs, clams, and shrimp call the reef home. So do other interesting creatures, such as sea cucumbers, anemones, and worms. About 2,000 different species live on the reef. Together they form a complex ecosystem.

⋔ This hawksbill turtle chomps on a meal of soft corals.

⊙ The parrot fish has a very sharp beak.

Since each coral polyp multiplies, what keeps the coral from growing too much? It may be the blue-green parrot fish. This fish is about the size and shape of a football. It has sharp teeth and a hard beak like a parrot's. Parrot fish eat coral polyps. They use their beaks to break off pieces of the hard coral shell. Then they use their teeth to grind the coral so they can get at the polyps. For them, this is just a meal. But it also keeps the coral in check.

Clown Fish and Anemone

Clown fish get their name from their striking coloring that resembles an orange clown suit with a white collar, cuffs, and socks. The anemone (uh-NEM-uh-nee) resembles a plant with wavy green stems, but it is actually a large polyp. The "stems" are its tentacles, and they sting. The clown fish and the anemone depend on each other. The anemone's stings do not hurt the clown fish, but they hurt other fish that prey on it. The anemone is rewarded by eating the scraps dropped by the clown fish when the clown fish eats.

ᴖ This photo shows a clown fish swimming among the tentacles of an anemone.

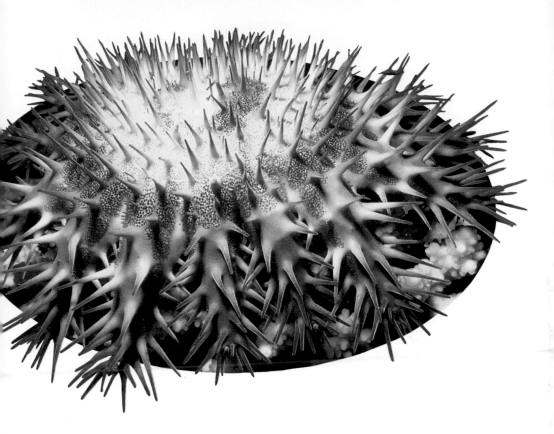

⌒ The crown-of-thorns starfish is one of the coral's main predators. They have damaged coral reefs by overeating.

The crown-of-thorns starfish eats polyps too. A starfish doesn't have teeth, so how does it eat the coral polyps? The starfish lies on top of the coral. Then it squeezes some of the digestive juices from its stomach onto the coral. The juice dissolves the polyp, and the starfish drinks the liquid.

↷ Scuba divers may see brightly colored fish like this one.

Another fish found in the reef is the cleaner wrasse (RAS). It eats parasites. Parasites are creatures that attach themselves to other organisms and live off them. One or two parasites might not hurt a host creature, but too many could kill it.

The small cleaner wrasse eats parasites that live on a fish. The cleaner wrasse moves around the fish's body, eating the little parasites from the scales, gills, and even inside its mouth.

Sea snakes glide in the warm waters around the reef. Sometimes crocodiles swim in from one of the many rivers that feed into the ocean along the reef.

Dugongs (DEW-gongz) are a type of sea cow similar to a manatee. These large, gentle plant eaters forage on the sea grass under the reef waters.

Seven species of sea turtle exist in the world. Six of them live in the Great Barrier Reef.

◔ The leatherback turtle hatchling swims in tropical waters.

Food for All

Everything that lives in the Great Barrier Reef depends on something else for survival. Small fish eat the grasses and seaweed. Larger fish eat the smaller fish.

whale

sea turtle   seahorse

Pipefish and seahorses feed on small fish and shellfish. The pipefish looks like a small, thin pipe. It's almost hard to believe it is a sea animal. The seahorse has a face that is long and pointed like a horse's. These creatures don't swim like fish or glide like sea snakes. They bob along in the water.

CHAPTER 3

A Valuable Resource

Coral itself is hard, but its ecosystem is fragile and needs to be preserved.

Scientists constantly check the Great Barrier Reef. They track the number and species of animals, and they keep tabs on any changes that occur.

They may find that a type of coral is not forming at its usual rate. Or they may find that the population of one kind of animal is getting smaller. This can mean that the reef is in danger. Scientists look at what may have caused the changes. Then they try to find a way to correct it.

⊍ Divers enjoy a spectacular view of the reef.

⌒ As long as the Great Barrier Reef is protected, this dugong calf will live a long life.

For example, scientists noticed that the number of dugongs was getting smaller. They wanted to find out why. There were many reasons. Some were getting caught in shark nets. Some were dying because their habitat was being ruined.

Plans were put into effect to change this. Dugong Protection Areas were created. Shark nets were outlawed. Other laws were passed to keep people from hunting and catching dugongs.

It will be a long time before we know if these steps have worked. Dugongs breed slowly. Only one calf is born every three years. Scientists will have to wait to see if the population increases.

In 1975 the government of Australia acted to preserve the Great Barrier Reef. It created the Great Barrier Reef Marine Park to protect most of the reef. In 1981 it was added to the United Nations list of World Heritage areas.

This means that people cannot do anything that might harm the reef. They must not fish, hunt, **harvest** coral, or dump chemicals into the water.

Coral Harvesting

Since coral is valuable, divers have harvested it for many years. The more they harvested, the more they were paid. If divers were to harvest too much coral, the reef would begin to disappear. Also, destroying the young polyps means that no new coral would grow. Now harvesting is against the law.

Conclusion

The Great Barrier Reef is one of nature's wonders. It is home to more species than any other place on Earth. Every year scientists discover new information about it.

Because of the efforts to save the reef, it will still exist for people who want to see it in the future. It will still be there for scientists who want to study it. And it will still be a place for millions of sea creatures to call home.

⊍ A diver sees the coral close-up.

Glossary

ecosystem *(EE-koh-sis-tuhm)* all the living and nonliving things in a certain area that depend on each other *(page 2)*

habitable *(HAB-it-uh-buhl)* to be able to live on or in something *(page 7)*

habitat *(HAB-i-tat)* the place where an animal or plant naturally lives and grows *(page 8)*

harvest *(HAR-vist)* gather a crop or other living thing *(page 17)*

limestone *(LIGHM-stohn)* a hard rock formed by polyps *(page 6)*

organic *(or-GAN-ik)* coming from living things *(page 2)*

population *(pop-yuh-LAY-shuhn)* the number of people or animals that live in an ecosystem *(page 8)*

species *(SPEE-sheez)* a group of plants or animals that are alike in certain ways *(page 7)*

Index

Aboriginal peoples, *3*

anemone, *10*

cleaner wrasse, *12*

clown fish, *10*

Cook, James, *4*

crown-of-thorns starfish, *11*

dugongs, *13, 16*

parrot fish, *9*

pipefish, *14*

polyps, *6, 9*

seahorse, *14*

Comprehension Check

Summarize

List some facts that you have learned about the Great Barrier Reef. Then write some opinions about the Great Barrier Reef too. Use the information to summarize what you learned from reading this book.

Think and Compare

1. Reread pages 5–6. What facts did you learn about coral? Write your opinions about coral. *(Evaluate Fact and Opinion)*

2. What other information would you like to know about the Great Barrier Reef? How can you find out more about it? *(Synthesize)*

3. Why is it important for people to learn about endangered areas? *(Evaluate)*